FINDING
GOD'S
FAVOR

HOW TO BRING MEANING AND
BLESSING INTO YOUR LIFE

*"For whoso
findeth me
findeth life,
and shall
obtain favour
of the Lord."*
—Proverbs 8:35

www.moretolife.info
THROUGH GOD'S WORD

Finding
GOD'S
FAVOR

HOW TO BRING MEANING AND BLESSING INTO YOUR LIFE

"For whoso findeth me findeth life, and shall obtain favour of the Lord."

—Proverbs 8:35

Finding God's Favor

by Gayla Baughman, Beth Dillon, Julie Long,
Mary Loudermilk

©2002, Word Aflame® Press
Hazelwood, MO 63042-2299

Cover Design by Paul Povolni

ISBN 0-75772-569-4

All Scripture quotations in this book are from the King James Version of
the Bible unless otherwise identified.

Printed in United States of America

Printed by

WORD AFLAME®PRESS
8855 DUNN ROAD
HAZELWOOD, MO 63042-2299

Contributing Writers

Gayla Baughman

Beth Dillon

Julie Long

Mary Loudermilk

Contents

www.moretolife.info
THROUGH GOD'S WORD

*"For whoso findeth me findeth life, and shall
obtain favour of the LORD."
Proverbs 8:35*

Introduction

Some time back on a cold, rainy day my parents drove me to the airport. I asked them just to drop me off so they wouldn't have to worry about parking the car and getting out in the rain. But my 70-year-old dad insisted on carrying my luggage inside the airport.

Once inside, I stated that I would be fine and suggested that he go ahead and leave. But again, he insisted on carrying my luggage through the line to the ticket counter, then over to the security table. He waited with me as they searched my luggage, then carried my luggage back over to the ticket counter and waited with me until they finally released my ticket to me. He walked me to the security entrance (as far

11

as he could go) and once he saw that I'd made it through, he went on his way.

I am no longer a little girl. I am a grown woman. But as we stood there that day I reflected on how wonderful it felt to be cared for by my father. His presence made me feel safe. His concern made me feel protected and cherished. His touch made me feel loved. Although I could have managed on my own, I was very glad that I didn't have to.

Much has been written about the relationship of a father and his daughter. A woman's self-esteem and confidence flow from a healthy father/daughter relationship. Much has also been written about how our relationships with our natural fathers affect the way we perceive our Heavenly Father. In my case, I have been blessed. The love of my natural father has helped me to be open to receive the love of my Heavenly Father. And as I crave the love, attention, and favor of my natural father, so I also have a deep desire to have the favor of my Heavenly Father.

Maybe your story doesn't read like mine. But the truth of the matter is, no matter what kind of relationship we've had with our natural fathers, we all have a Heavenly Father who loves us and wants His best for our lives. You may feel as if you are living life on your own with no one to look out for you but yourself. But it doesn't have to be that way any more. You have a Heavenly Father who cares.

It is my desire that through the pages of this study, *Finding God's Favor*, you will come to know your Heavenly Father in a new and more intimate way. His Word promises that if we seek Him with our whole heart, we will find Him: "And ye shall seek me, and find me, when ye shall search for me with all your heart" (Jeremiah 29:13).

So let's begin right now. . . .

Lesson 1

Needing God's Favor

Life Focus

Every person needs the favor of God. We need God's blessings every day. It is a privilege to be favored by God. The favor of God is the fountain of all good.

"It is of the LORD'S mercies that we are not consumed, because his compassions fail not. They are new every morning: great is thy faithfulness" (Lamentations 3:22-23).

"Every good gift and every perfect gift is from above, and cometh down from the Father of lights, with whom is no variableness, neither shadow of turning" (James 1:17).

A Look at the Word

So that we both/or all have the same understanding of the word *"favor,"* let's read how it is defined:

> **Favor:** OBLIGE: to do a kindness for; ENDOW: to treat gently or carefully; SPARE: refrain from harming; PREFER: to show partiality toward; SUSTAIN: to give support or confirmation to; FACILITATE: to afford advantages for success to.

From the creation of mankind, God has always favored or blessed those men and women who were obedient to His commands. Let's take a quick look at just a few who are mentioned in the Bible (emphasis added).

> ✍ "And Abel, he also brought of the firstlings of his flock and of the fat thereof. And the LORD had *respect* unto Abel and to his offering" (Genesis 4:4).

Life Reflection

The Lord had *respect* for Abel. We all wish to be respected by those around us—our husband, children, family, friends, and peers. Do you feel respected as a person? As a wife? As a mother? As a friend? As a daughter? As an employee?

CR "And Enoch walked with God: and he was not; for *God took him*" (Genesis 5:24). "By faith Enoch was translated that he should not see death; and was not found, because God had translated him: for before his translation he had this testimony, that *he pleased God*" (Hebrews 11:5).

Life Reflection

Enoch was pleasing to God. What a testimony—to be pleasing to God. As children we desire to please our parents. As adults we desire to please others around us—our husband, children, employer, etc. In the same way, we should desire to be pleasing to God. Do you have that desire? Discuss ways to become pleasing to God.

CR "But Noah found *grace* in the eyes of the LORD" (Genesis 6:8).

CR "Now the LORD had said unto Abram, Get thee out of thy country, and from thy kindred, and from thy father's house, unto a land that I will shew thee: and I will

17

make of thee a great nation, and I will bless thee, and make thy name great; and thou shalt be a blessing: and I will bless them that bless thee, and curse him that curseth thee: and in thee shall all families of the earth be blessed" (Genesis 12:1-3).

What a tall order! God told Abraham to leave all he had ever known. However, because of Abraham's obedience to God's command, all of God's promises to him were fulfilled.

Life Reflection

Obedience is not always easy, but it is rewarding. Can you think back to times in your life when obedience was difficult, but you were rewarded for it?

Because of Abraham's obedience, he was blessed by God and became the father of the nation of Israel. (See Genesis 17:1-5.) God then extended His favor beyond a single man, individually, to an entire nation.

Let's read Deuteronomy 7:6-8 together.

"For thou art an holy people unto the LORD thy God: the LORD thy God hath chosen thee to be a special people unto himself, above all people that are upon the face of the earth.

"The LORD did not set his love upon you, nor choose you, because ye were more in number than any people; for ye were the fewest of all people:

"But because the LORD loved you, and because he would keep the oath which he had sworn unto your fathers, hath the LORD brought you out with a mighty hand, and redeemed you out of the house of bondmen, from the hand of Pharaoh king of Egypt."

God promises us great deliverance from things in our lives that have tormented us or kept us bound—spiritually, physically, or emotionally—if we are in obedience to Him and have His favor. Because of God's favor upon the Israelite nation, He brought them out of Egypt, through the wilderness, and into the Promised Land. The following passages capsule the history of the Israelite nation:

"We have heard with our ears, O God, our fathers have told us, what work thou didst in their days, in the times of old.

"How thou didst drive out the heathen with thy hand, and plantedst them; how thou didst afflict the people, and cast them out.

"For they got not the land in possession by their own sword, neither did their

19

own arm save them: but thy right hand, and thine arm, and the light of thy countenance, because thou hadst a favour unto them" (Psalm 44:1-3).

The Israelite people needed the favor of God. They acknowledged that they did not gain the Promised Land by their own sword, nor were they saved by their own arm, but only by the favor of God. Review quickly the definition of favor at the beginning of this lesson. Read below to see how God fulfilled this definition by showing His favor to the nation of Israel. He:

- **Delivered** them (from Egyptian bondage, servitude).
- **Provided** for them (manna, water, clothes, shoes).
- **Obliged** them (quail).
- **Sustained** them (strength, stamina, health).
- **Facilitated** them (victory in battles).
- **Endowed** them (love, mercy, forgiveness for disobedience).
- **Preferred** them (chosen, special people).
- **Spared** them (from wrath, judgment, annihilation).

God's favor will bring the same results in your life!

The Word in My Life

Wouldn't you love to have the favor of God in your life on a daily basis?

- ❧ To know that whatever you need, God would provide. (See Philippians 4:19.)
- ❧ To know that He would be there to strengthen and sustain you. (See Psalm 55:22.)
- ❧ To know that He would endow you with His love, mercy, and forgiveness. (See Lamentations 3:22-23.)
- ❧ To know that He would prefer you as His chosen friend. (See John 15:13-16.)

Numbers 6:22-27 relates the special blessing that God gave to the Israelite nation, which can be your blessing as well. Let's read it together:

> "And the LORD spake unto Moses, saying, Speak unto Aaron and unto his sons, saying, On this wise ye shall bless the children of Israel, saying unto them, the LORD bless thee, and keep thee: the LORD make his face shine upon thee, and be gracious unto thee: the LORD lift up his countenance upon thee, and give thee peace. And they shall put my name upon the children of Israel; and I will bless them."

21

In this passage we see the favor of His face, the favor of His grace, and the favor of His peace. Let's look at each one a little more closely.

The Favor of His Face *(Protection from evil—oblige/endow)*

Life Reflection

Can you remember a time when you felt your natural father's approval? Didn't it make you feel loved and accepted? Have you ever felt the approval of your Heavenly Father? He wants you to feel His love and acceptance.

Read: Psalm 27:8-10 (Father to those forsaken by father)

Psalm 68:5 (Father to the fatherless)

Psalm 103:13 (As a father pities his children, so the Lord pities them that fear Him.)

ભ **The Lord lift up His countenance upon you.** "The Lord look on you with favor" (NKJV). We can understand this statement more clearly by envisioning a father smiling down upon his child, or a man or woman smiling with delight upon seeing a special friend. Do you long for the approving smile of a Father?

God is your Father and He is smiling down upon you right now.

> ⚘ **The Lord make His face shine upon you.** This phrase can be paralleled to the sun shining upon the earth, bringing light and renewing life through the warmth of its rays. Do you crave the warmth of your Father's love?
> Read: I John 4:9-10; Romans 8:37-39. God's love is unconditional and eternal. Nothing can ever separate you from the love of God, your Father.

The Favor of His Grace *(Pardon from sin—spare/prefer)*

God wants to bless you, to keep you, and to show His amazing grace to you.

> ⚘ **The Lord bless you** (Deuteronomy 28:1-14). His blessings come as we listen to His voice and obey His commandments.

     ❧ ***The Lord keep you*** (II Thessalonians 3:3; Jude 24). God promises to establish us, keep us from evil, and keep us from falling.

     ❧ ***The Lord be gracious to you*** (Ephesians 2:4-8). He offers us His love, mercy, kindness, and grace. We do not earn this; it is a gift from Him.

Life Reflection

Is there an area of your life into which you would like the Lord to bring peace? Is there a family situation that needs a touch of His peace? Do you feel uncertain in your spiritual walk and need His assurance about your relationship with Him? Do world events distress you and cause worry and stress?

Jesus once spoke to the storm and said, "Peace, be still" (Mark 4:39). Whatever the situation, God can step into your time of storm and speak peace to the waves that overflow you. God desires you to have a life that is filled with peace.

The Favor of His Peace *(Provision of peace—sustain/facilitate)*

God wants to bless you with personal peace, spiritual peace, and national peace.

⚘ *The Lord give you peace.*

The Lord wants to give you *personal peace* (Psalm 29:11; 119:165). You may feel the need for personal peace concerning: safety and serenity (Psalm 4:8); finances and health (III John 2); peace from the battles of life, whether family, job, or other situations (Psalm 55:18); and peace from enemies (Proverbs 16:7).

The Lord wants to give you *spiritual peace* (Romans 14:17; Isaiah 26:3). This means you can possess the fullness of peace (Philippians 4:7), the peace that comes as the fruit of the Spirit (Galatians 5:22), and peace that brings freedom from fear (John 14:27).

The Lord also can bring *national peace* to our land: security, tranquility, amity (Psalm 147:14).

Life Reflection

Do you recognize the need for God's favor in your life? Let's read Proverbs 3:1-4 to find more about obtaining God's favor for our lives:

"My son, forget not my law; but let thine heart keep my commandments: for length of days, and long life, and peace, shall they add to thee. Let not mercy and truth forsake thee: bind them about thy neck; write them upon the table of thine heart: so shalt thou find favour and good under-standing in the sight of God and man."

List the things the Bible instructs us to do to find the favor of God.

List the blessings mentioned in this passage that you will receive for your obedience.

A Prayer from the Word

Pray the following prayer that David prayed in Psalm 31.

"Turn your ear to me, come quickly to my rescue; be my rock of refuge, a strong fortress to save me. Since you are my rock and my fortress, for the sake of your name lead and guide me. Free me from the trap that is set for me, for you are my refuge.

"Into your hands I commit my spirit; redeem me, O LORD the God of truth. I will be glad and rejoice in your love, for you saw my affliction and knew the anguish of my soul. My times are in your hands; deliver me from my enemies and from those who pursue me.

"Let your face shine on your servant; save me in your unfailing love. How great is your goodness, which you have stored up for those who fear you, which you bestow in the sight of men on those who take refuge in you" (Portions of Psalm 31, NIV).

૭૩

More to Life . . . for this week

Memorize these verses: Lamentations 3:22-23

Read this passage: Psalm 42

Answer this question: In what way did the writer of this Psalm express his need of God? Do you ever feel so empty that you actually hunger or thirst for something to fill that emptiness? Do you ever feel cast down in your soul? Disquieted? Psalm 42:8 tells you that "the LORD will command his lovingkindness in the daytime, and in the night his song shall be with me." God is the answer to the emptiness in your life. He is the health and the hope of your countenance. Night or day, He is available and accessible.

Apply this to your life: Make a list of the areas in your life in which you see the greatest need for God's favor or divine intervention. Pray over this list at least once each day. If you feel comfortable, share the list with your Bible study partner so that she can agree with you in prayer. (Read Matthew 18:19.)

We have just begun our journey to find God's favor. Let's continue on to the next lesson that instructs us on how to seek the favor of God.

Lesson 2

Seeking God's Favor

Life Focus

Every person should seek the favor of God. We should seek God's divine intervention for our needs.

"I intreated thy favour with my whole heart: be merciful unto me according to thy word" (Psalm 119:58).

"He shall call upon me, and I will answer him: I will be with him in trouble; I will deliver him, and honour him" (Psalm 91:15).

A Look at the Word

Although all of us really want the favor of God, we often do not know how to seek that favor in our daily lives. A beautiful story from the Old Testament Book of Esther can help us understand God's willingness to bring favor or grace into our lives. Though the word *God* is never used in the Book of Esther, the favor of

God was on Esther's life, just as it can be upon ours.

Esther was a lovely young Jewish girl living in exile in the land of Babylon. Her parents both dead, Mordecai, her cousin, cared for the girl. She and Mordecai lived in Shushan, the palace (capital city) of King Ahasuerus. After Queen Vashti angered the king and was then dethroned, the king's officers set out to find a new queen from among the fairest virgins of the land. One of the maidens selected to be brought to court was Esther, the Jewish orphan girl. Obeying the advice of Mordecai, she remained silent about her ancestry.

For twelve months Esther went through a purification process in anticipation of her presentation to the king. During this time of preparation, she found the favor of those around her.

- ❧ She immediately found favor with Hegai, the keeper of the women, who gave her preferential treatment during this time of preparation (Esther 2:9).
- ❧ Others also noticed the lovely Jewish girl: "And Esther obtained favour in the sight of all them that looked upon her" (Esther 2:15).
- ❧ Most importantly, she found the favor of the king. Perhaps her beauty was

no greater than that of other maidens, but something in her demeanor set her apart. "And the king loved Esther above all the women, and she obtained grace and favour in his sight more than all the virgins; so that he set the royal crown upon her head, and made her queen instead of Vashti" (Esther 2:17).

Life Reflection

What qualities do you think Esther displayed that caused her to receive the favor of the king and others around her? What qualities can we develop in our lives to help us find favor with friends, family, neighbors or coworkers? What qualities do you think God would like to see us develop in our lives?

A time came when all that stood between the Jews and destruction was a young orphan girl who now reigned as queen. An enemy of her people sought to annihilate them, but God used Esther to defeat this wicked plan. Mordecai felt she had "come to the kingdom for such a time as this." After fasting and

31

prayer, she entered the presence of the king without first being summonsed, a fearful and forbidden thing to do in the court. However, the need was too great to consider her own safety.

"If I have found favour in thy sight, O king, and if it please the king, let my life be given me at my petition, and my people at my request" (Esther 7:3).

The king's favor upon Esther brought deliverance to her and her people and destruction to the enemy.

The Book of Esther ends with this courageous queen writing a decree that these events never be forgotten and that the memorial of Purim continue every year. She "wrote with all authority . . . and the decree of Esther confirmed these matters of Purim" (Esther 9:29, 32). She became a person of influence in the kingdom and with the people of God. To this day, Purim is still celebrated by Jewish people.

(For the full story of Esther's role in helping her people, read the Book of Esther, a short book of the Bible.)

Life Reflection

Fear could have stopped Esther from approaching the king without first being summonsed into his presence. But her need was greater than her fear. Do you feel uncertain or fearful of bringing your requests to God? Think of needs in your life that you would like to bring to Him. Then take this verse for your very own: "Let us therefore come boldly unto the throne of grace, that we may obtain mercy, and find grace to help in time of need" (Hebrews 4:16).

The Word in My Life

One reason some people are reluctant to approach God is because they do not feel good enough to ask Him for help. By nature we are sinful, so we think that God will not accept us. But this is where His favor—or grace—steps in. Grace is not something we earn but it is given "just because." It is God's unmerited (undeserved) favor. A gift.

"But God commendeth his love toward us, in that, while we were yet sinners,

Christ died for us. . . . But where sin abounded, grace did much more abound: that as sin hath reigned unto death, even so might grace reign through righteousness unto eternal life by Jesus Christ our Lord" (Romans 5:8, 20-21).

Life Reflection

Sometimes we feel that we have to be a certain way or do a certain thing to earn the love of those around us. Their actions, if not their words, say, "I'll love you if. . . ." Can you think of times when you felt that you fell short of another's expectations? Did you feel they loved you less? Did you think that you could never do quite enough to earn their love?

God's love is unconditional. He loves us as we are—warts, wrinkles, and all—and reaches out to help us reach our potential. His love is not of the "I'll love you if" variety, but is "I'll love you regardless of. . . ."

How can we think of all that God has done without thankfulness and wonder rising in our hearts!

34

CR He loved us before we were lovable.

CR He died in our place.

CR He gives grace (favor) greater than our sin.

CR He promises eternal life.

During His ministry on earth, Jesus was often criticized for associating with those of a poor reputation. He did not hesitate to reach out to or even socialize with people considered with little regard by others. One such incident is told in Luke 7:36-50 when a woman of low reputation washed Jesus' feet with her tears, wiped them with her hair, kissed them, and finally anointed them with precious ointment.

The observers said, "This man, if he were a prophet, would have known who and what manner of woman this is that toucheth him: for she is a sinner" (verse 39). Jesus condemned them by relating a parable of two debtors whose debts, one small and one great, were forgiven. He pointed out that the one forgiven the most, loved the most. To the woman He said, "Thy sins are forgiven . . . Thy faith hath saved thee; go in peace" (verses 48, 50).

This woman, though a sinner, found favor and forgiveness in the eyes of Jesus because she came with an attitude of humility and worship. She was willing to bear the scorn of those around her for the opportunity to demonstrate her love of Jesus. As a result, her sins were forgiven. "In my favour have I had mercy on thee" (Isaiah 60:10).

When we seek God wholeheartedly, we are expressing our desire to establish a relationship with Him. He is quick to reciprocate, wanting that relationship with us as well. He promises that as we move toward Him, He moves even closer to us.

> ☙ "And ye shall seek me, and find me, when ye shall search for me with all your heart" (Jeremiah 29:13).
> ☙ "Draw nigh to God, and he will draw nigh to you" (James 4:8).
> ☙ "The LORD is nigh unto all them that call upon him . . . he also will hear their cry, and will save them" (Psalm 145:18-19).

Life Reflection

Back in the days before seatbelt laws and bucket seats, a couple who were married for several years was traveling down the highway, the husband driving and the wife thinking. Feeling perhaps that her husband didn't show as much affection for her as he once did, the wife began to reminisce. "Remember when we were first married and would drive along sitting real close to each other?" The husband quickly responded with one short sentence. "I didn't move."

Do you feel that God is not as close to you as He once was or as you would like Him to be? Who moved? What action of yours can improve the relationship and draw you closer together?

The secret to any close relationship is good communication. A couple in love may talk for hours at a time, and it seems just a few moments. During this time they are discovering each other's inner thoughts and feelings. It is a mutual sharing of the deep things of the heart. Without this time of discovery, the relationship stays shallow and superficial. If communication stops, the relationship will wither and die.

Life Reflection

What is the difference between a good friend and an acquaintance? Can you think of a close friend who moved away? Were you able to maintain that same level of friendship? Or did you gradually drift apart? How would you go about restoring a lost friendship?

How would you rate the quality of your relationship with Jesus Christ? Are you close? Are you willing to share your deep thoughts and desires with Him? Or is He just an acquaintance?

C3 Prayer is our source of communication with God. (Read Zechariah 13:9.)

C3 When we pray, our purpose should be to learn more about God, to discover His glory and greatness. (Read Colossians 1:9-10.)

C3 We can also "pray the Word," reciting portions of Scripture that reveal how great God is and how He cares for us. (Psalm 145:1-3.)

"Evening, and morning, and at noon, will I pray, and cry aloud: and he shall hear my voice" (Psalm 55:17).

Other qualities also deepen a relationship. We discover three important attributes that help us draw closer to God when we read Psalm 37:4-5.

"*Delight* thyself also in the LORD; and he shall give thee the desires of thine heart. *Commit* thy way unto the LORD; *trust* also in him; and he shall bring it to pass" (emphasis added).

CB When we *delight* in someone, we seek to please him. We enjoy being around that person and treasure our times together. We want to make him happy and refrain from any actions that would damage the relationship.

CB When we *commit* ourselves to someone, we are making a promise or pledge. We are dedicating ourselves to making the relationship last. We feel serious about it. A committed relationship speaks of permanency.

CB When we *trust* someone, we place our faith and confidence in him. We find that person to be trustworthy—honest and reliable. We know that person will be true to us and will seek only our good. We can count on him; he does not break promises.

As we develop our prayer life, our lines of communication, we will find joy and delight in conversing with God. As we commit to serve Him, He commits to meet our every need. We learn that He is trustworthy, and we can count on the promises we read in His Word.

As we seek God and His favor in our lives, we learn that He will guide our steps and help us to reach our greatest potential in Him.

"In all thy ways acknowledge him, and he shall direct thy paths" (Proverbs 3:6).

"I will instruct thee and teach thee in the way which thou shalt go: I will guide thee with mine eye" (Psalm 32:8).

"Being confident of this very thing, that he which hath begun a good work in you will perform it until the day of Jesus Christ" (Philippians 1:6).

Life Reflection

What "good work" would you like to see God perform in your life? Are you willing to trust Him to direct the path of your life into the place He chooses, knowing that it will be the best direction for you?

A Prayer from the Word

Lord, I am willing for You to instruct me, teach me, and guide me. I will delight in You, commit to You, and trust You as my closest Friend. Help me to follow Your leading when I make decisions for my life and help me to learn to inquire of Your best plan for me before I act. Thank You, Lord Jesus, for being there for me every day. I seek Your grace and favor on my life.

ભ

More to Life . . . for this week

Memorize this verse: Psalm 91:15

Read this passage: Daniel 6

Answer this question: How important was Daniel's daily communication with God? Did he allow circumstances to deter him from his commitment to his God? Did God hear his prayers? Is daily communication with God important to you? Do you make time to seek God for your own needs and the needs of others?

Apply this to your life: Make a commitment to seek God every day this week for a certain amount of time and at a certain place. For example: five minutes every morning kneeling by your bedside; ten minutes a day on your lunch break sitting in your car; or fifteen minutes every evening walking around your block. The time, position, or place does not matter— just that you make a commitment and keep it. Proverbs 8:17 says: "I love those who love me, and those who seek me find me" (NIV). Your Heavenly Father would love for you to communicate with Him on a daily basis. If you need help keeping your commitment, ask your Bible study partner to check up on you.

Not only can we seek God's favor upon our lives, but we can also feel His favor through the infilling of His Spirit. Let's read on to find out more.

Feeling God's Favor

Life Focus

Everyone can feel the favor of God. You can feel the presence of God in your life through repentance, water baptism in the name of Jesus, and the infilling of the Holy Ghost—the Spirit of God dwelling in you.

"That they should seek the Lord, if haply they might feel after him, and find him, though he be not far from every one of us" (Acts 17:27).

"Then Peter said unto them, Repent, and be baptized every one of you in the name of Jesus Christ for the remission of sins, and ye shall receive the gift of the Holy Ghost" (Acts 2:38).

A Look at the Word

A four-year-old girl became frightened by a tremendous thunderstorm one evening.

After one loud clap of thunder, she jumped out of bed, ran down the hallway to her parents' bedroom, and jumped right in between her mom and dad. Her father tried to calm her fears by saying that God would look after her. The daughter replied, "I know that, Daddy, but right now I need someone with skin on!"

Have you ever felt that way about God? If only I could feel Him. How do I know for certain that my life has the approval of God? These feelings are universal because the greatest human need is to feel accepted. We are in a lifelong pursuit for a tangible way to fulfill this need.

We crave relationships in which we are accepted, valued, and wanted; but we seldom experience the "real thing." We have believed the lie that says our value is determined by the quality and level of our performance.

How can we end this futile quest and experience real, unconditional love? The answer is in the unwarranted, undeserved, unearned favor of God. God invites you to feel His favor—favor "with skin on!"

Mary, the mother of Jesus, is arguably the best known of all women in the Bible. Her name is recognized around the world, and the importance of her role in history is widely acknowledged. She was the first to hear that God was about to break into history with the birth of the Messiah, her son-to-be, and Mary was the first to hear His name, Jesus. The

44

name Jesus is explained in Matthew 1:21: "For he shall save his people from their sins." Jesus came to offer humanity the ultimate favor of God—salvation!

Let's quickly review the story as related in Luke 1:26-56. Mary, a young woman with no great social standing or wealth, was promised in marriage to a carpenter named Joseph. One day as she went about her daily routine, an angel appeared and said, "Hail, thou that art highly favoured, the Lord is with thee: blessed art thou among women." The angel told her that she had been chosen to carry Jesus Christ, the Savior of the world. All of humanity would receive an extraordinary gift through her.

Mary's response was: "Be it unto me according to thy word." She didn't say, "Let me think about this," or "I'll get back to you later," or "I'm extremely busy for the next nine months, try again another time." Mary simply said yes to God and His plan for her life. Salvation became available to all humanity because of her trust and obedience. She accepted God's touch upon her life.

The last mention of Mary in the Bible pictures her with other believers praying in Jerusalem after the resurrection of Jesus, waiting for the coming of the Holy Spirit (Acts 1:14).

Let's look closer at why Mary "found favour with God," how she felt the favor of God, and the result of God's favor in her life.

Mary's Preparation

During Mary's time of preparation, before she felt the favor of God, we can observe several qualities in her life.

       ᘓ ***Humility.*** Probably in her early teens, the typical age for engagement in first-century Galilee, Mary had never thought of herself as extraordinary. No doubt she worshiped God and held onto the slim hope, as did every Jewish woman, that she might be chosen to bear the Messiah. But she wouldn't have used words like "highly favoured" and "blessed . . . among women" to describe herself. Mary simply saw herself as a person who loved God and was privileged to serve Him any way she could.

       ᘓ ***Faith.*** "How shall this be?" Mary questioned (verse 34). She spoke out of curiosity, not doubt. We may assume that she felt embarrassment at being pregnant while unmarried. The angel responded, "The Holy Ghost shall come upon thee, and the power of the Highest shall overshadow thee" (verse 35). Mary's simple faith and readiness to do God's will brought the blessing of God into her life (verse 45).

Obedience. The questions that Mary did *not* ask are significant. Questions like: "What will Joseph think?" "What will people think of me?" "What will happen to me?" Under the circumstances we wouldn't be surprised if Mary had wavered at this point. If these questions ran through her mind, she quickly dismissed them. Instead she expressed her obedience: "Be it unto me according to thy word." She placed her social position, her marriage, even her way of life in jeopardy for the sake of God's will.

Life Reflection

If your life was suddenly interrupted by an angel's announcement, what do you think your reaction might be? Would you become excited? Shocked? Reluctant? A little of each?

If God told you today that He had a special plan for your life, how would you react? Acceptance? Happiness? Fear or doubt? Do you feel you can completely trust Him and that He wants only the best for your life?

Mary's Confirmation

Mary received confirmation of God's favor in her life from several different sources:

℘ ***God's Messenger.*** God confirmed His will through His messenger, Gabriel (verse 26). The angel announced, "Hail, thou that art highly favoured, the Lord is with thee: blessed art thou among women. . . . Fear not, Mary, for thou hast found favour with God." God had already extended His favor to Mary before she had surrendered to His plan, but her only proof at this point was the word of the angel, God's messenger.

℘ ***Inward Confirmation.*** "The Holy Ghost shall come upon thee, and the power of the Highest shall overshadow thee" (verse 35). The word "overshadow" means to envelop. What was going to take place in Mary's life was a direct act of God; the power of the Most High, the Holy Spirit, would wrap around and "overshadow" her. Overshadowing suggests the hovering presence of God. "The Lord is with thee" (verse 28).

℘ ***Outward Confirmation.*** Elizabeth, who was filled with the Holy Ghost, confirmed the favor of God on Mary's life. "Blessed art thou among women, and blessed is the fruit of thy womb" (verses 41-42). She recognized through supernatural illumination and understanding that Mary was carrying the Messiah—the Savior of the world!

Mary's Participation

After the confirmation of God's favor in her life, Mary was filled with joy, and she expressed herself in one of the most beautiful songs of praise ever recorded (verses 46-55).

ɷ *Praise.* Mary rejoiced in what God had done in her life and what He was going to do for coming generations (verses 46-47). To magnify means to enlarge or amplify. When Mary received the confirmation of the Holy Spirit in her life, her response was for her life to draw attention to God—to make God larger.

ɷ *Witness*. Because of the inward sign, the newborn life within her, Mary now knew the holiness, the mercy, the might, and the faithfulness of God (verses 49-55). The touch of the Holy Ghost caused her to erupt in perfect praise and thanksgiving to God.

49

The Word in My Life

What blessing do I need most from God? How can I feel the favor of God in my life? The Holy Ghost is God's approval, acceptance, and blessing on our life. The Holy Ghost is the very real presence of God that we can feel. When we receive the Holy Ghost, we become part of God's family; we belong, we matter, we are accepted. We are no longer outcasts or second-class citizens; we are part of His family.

Let's apply the lessons we learned from the life of Mary to determine how we too can feel the presence of God!

My Preparation

How do I prepare myself to feel the favor of God?

Favor can be interpreted as surprising grace. If we want to feel the grace of God as Mary did, we must possess the same qualities—faith, humility, and obedience.

     Faith—Believe the Word of God. The first step toward feeling the favor of God is to believe what the Bible teaches. Romans 3:23 says, "All have sinned, and come short of the glory of God." Humanity lost favor with God because of sin, but through Jesus Christ we can be reconnected to God.

50

Romans 5:8 says, "God commendeth his love toward us, in that, while we were yet sinners, Christ died for us."

Hebrews 11:6 tells us, "Without faith it is impossible to please him." Faith is taking God at His Word, trusting Him, and obeying His Word.

Life Reflection

What did Jesus Christ do to make it possible for me to feel God's favor?

Why do I need faith to feel the favor of God?

Humility—Repent of My Sins. The second step toward feeling the favor of God is repentance. We know that there is a step beyond simply believing. Paul told the believers he met in Ephesus that they also needed to be baptized and to receive the Holy Ghost (Acts 19:1-6).

You may ask, "How could God love me? If God knew the real me, He wouldn't want to give His favor to me." The good news is that God does know you and you can still feel His favor. II Peter 3:9 says that God is "not willing that any should perish, but that all should come to repentance." Repentance is true humility. When we realize who God is and what we are, we ask for forgiveness and turn away from our old life to a new life in Christ.

Life Reflection

Why isn't belief in Jesus enough to bring the favor of God into my life?

What is repentance?

Obedience—Water Baptism in the Name of Jesus. After you have believed and repented, the next step toward feeling the favor of God is water baptism in the name of Jesus.

The word *baptize* means to immerse, and the first century church fulfilled the command of Jesus regarding water baptism by immersing believers in the name of Jesus.

The proper way to be baptized is in the name of Jesus: "Neither is there salvation in any other: for there is none other name under heaven given among men, whereby we must be saved" (Acts 4:12).

Life Reflection

Why do I need to be baptized by immersion in the name of Jesus to feel the favor of God? (Read Matthew 3:16; Mark 16:15-16; Acts 2:38, 41; Acts 8:12, 38-39; Acts 10:47-48; Acts 19:5.)

What are the three steps I need to take to prepare myself to receive the favor of God in my life?

My Confirmation—
When Will I Feel the Favor of God?

After you have repented and are obedient to God's Word regarding water baptism in the name of Jesus, you're ready for the confirmation of God's favor on your life—the Holy Spirit. (Read Ephesians 1:13.)

> ℭℨ ***God's Messenger.*** The Bible is God's message to humanity. God speaks to us through His written Word (II Timothy 2:15). God also communicates with us through the spoken Word. Romans 10:14 states, "How then shall they call on him in whom they have not believed? and how shall they believe in him of whom they have not heard? and how shall they hear without a preacher?"

Life Reflection

How does God communicate with me today?

ɕℨ *Inward Confirmation.* The Bible tells us in John 4:24 that God is a Spirit and often refers to God using the terms Holy Ghost or Holy Spirit. An individual can actually feel the power of God dwelling inside. The Holy Spirit will give you the power to live a new life. It is the guarantee of your inheritance of eternal life—feeling the favor of God for endless ages!

Perhaps you have asked yourself a question similar to Mary's, "How shall this be?" How do I experience the power of God in my life? In John 3:1-8 a man named Nicodemus puzzled over the statement of Jesus: "Except a man be born again, he cannot see the kingdom of God." To the many questions Nicodemus posed, Jesus gave this answer: "Except a man be born of *water* and of the *Spirit*, he cannot enter into the kingdom of God" (emphasis added).

These verses of Scripture show us that being born of the water in baptism and being born of the Spirit by receiving the Holy Ghost are necessary for salvation—the ultimate feeling of God's favor!

Life Reflection

What is the Holy Ghost? (Read Ephesians 1:13-14; John 14:15-20.)

How do I know that the Holy Ghost is necessary for salvation? (Read John 4:24; John 3:3-8; Romans 8:9-11.)

In the Book of Acts chapter 2, verse 37, the people questioned Peter and the apostles, "Men and brethren, what shall we do?" This question followed the outpouring of God's Spirit on the Day of Pentecost (Acts 2:1-4). The crowd of people that witnessed this event asked the apostle Peter how they too could experience this blessing from God. Peter answered:

"Repent, and be baptized every one of you in the name of Jesus Christ for the remission of sins, and ye shall receive the gift of the Holy Ghost. For the promise is unto you, and to your children, and to all that are afar off, even as many as the Lord our God shall call" (Acts 2:38-39).

Life Reflection

How do I know the Holy Ghost is for me today?

∞ ***Outward Confirmation.*** Speaking with tongues as God's Spirit gives the utterance is the first physical sign of the Holy Spirit in your life (Acts 2:4; Acts 10:45-46; Acts 19:6). Like the confirmation that Elizabeth gave to Mary concerning what God had done in her, speaking with tongues is the confirmation to you and to others that you have been filled with the Holy Spirit.

The favor of God was no more readily apparent in Mary's life than in Acts 1:14. The Bible tells us that Mary, the mother of Jesus, was in the upper room waiting for the promise of the Holy Ghost. The favor of God was upon her as the mother of Jesus, but far greater was the favor she received in her obedience to become a follower of Jesus. Mary was filled with the Holy Ghost!

Life Reflection

If you have not yet felt the favor of God, you have missed the greatest gift ever given—the gift of the Holy Spirit. God delights in you and desires to dwell in you.

How will I know that I have received the Holy Ghost? (Read Acts 2:4; Acts 10:45-46; Acts 19:6.)

My Participation. What Will Happen After I Feel the Favor of God?

೧ *Praise.* A fitting response to the Holy Spirit in your life is praise. To understand God's love for you and to feel His favor in your life brings spontaneous, eruptive praise to the One who offers unconditional acceptance!

Witness. Your life will be filled with joy that will overflow to others. Just like Mary, feeling the favor of God involves bearing Jesus. We must take Jesus to others who have not yet experienced His gracious acceptance (Acts 1:8).

Life Reflection

After I have felt the favor of God through the infilling of the Holy Ghost, what does God require of me? (Read Acts 1:8; Acts 4:33; Romans 14:17.)

A Prayer from the Word of God

Lord, help me to seek You, to feel after You, and to find You. I know that You are not far from me (Acts 17:27). I have read in Your Word that the gift of Your Spirit is for me (Acts 2:39). I want to respond to Your will for my life as Mary responded to You: "Be it unto me according to thy word."

> ℃
>
> *More to Life . . . for this week*
>
> **Memorize these verses:** Acts 2:38-39
>
> **Read this passage:** Acts 10
>
> **Answer this question:** Did God hear the prayers of Cornelius? Did Cornelius receive the gift of the Holy Ghost? Was he baptized in Jesus' name?
>
> **Apply this to your life:** By now you know that God is your loving Father Who hears and answers your prayers. Your Heavenly Father wants only the best for your life, and He "is no respecter of persons" (Acts 10:34). Continue to seek Him daily. As you pray, repent of any wrongdoing in word or deed; then ask your Father for His gift of the Holy Ghost. If you ask Him, He will give it to you. (Read Matthew 7:7-11.) When you receive the gift of the Holy Ghost, you will speak in an unknown tongue, as God's Spirit gives you the ability. (Read Acts 2:4.) If you have not been baptized in Jesus' name, make a decision to do so in obedience to God's Word.

Isn't it exciting to experience God's favor through the New Testament plan of salvation? Did you know that we can keep God's favor upon our lives daily? Let's continue on to Lesson 4 to find out how.

Lesson 4

Keeping God's Favor

Life Focus

Everyone must keep the favor of God. The presence of God will enable us to triumph in every circumstance or situation.

"Now thanks be unto God, which always causeth us to triumph in Christ, and maketh manifest the savour of his knowledge by us in every place" (II Corinthians 2:14).

A Look at the Word

It is not enough to feel God's favor every once in awhile, or just on special occasions; it is something we need to keep in and on our lives continually. You may still be wondering if it is possible for you to have God's favor each and every day of your life. The answer is yes!

When you receive the gift of the Holy Ghost with the biblical sign of speaking in tongues, you are filled with God's Spirit. The

Spirit of God within you then enables you to live in obedience to His Word—conducting yourself according to His will, not according to your own will. Continual obedience to God brings His continual blessing and favor upon your life.

This does not mean that every circumstance in your life will be perfect, but that through every circumstance and situation God will be with you and will help you through it.

Life Reflection

Have you encountered any difficulties lately? Are the circumstances in your life less than perfect right now? Read the following scriptures from the Word of God for strength and encouragement: Isaiah 41:10; Psalm 37:25, 39; Psalm 46:1-3; Psalm 55:22; and I Peter 3:12.

Sometimes God allows difficulties to come into our lives that we do not understand at the time, but He uses them to ultimately bring His blessings to us. The Bible teaches us that God's ways are above our ways, and Romans 8:28 gives us the promise that "all things work together for good to them that love God, to

them who are the called according to his purpose." The Old Testament story of Joseph,
found in Genesis 37-45, beautifully illustrates
this principle. Let's look at it together.

Joseph was the second to the youngest of
twelve brothers. The Bible tells us that
Joseph's father loved him more than his other
children because he was the son of his old age
(Genesis 37:3). The obvious favoritism of his
father caused much jealousy among Joseph's
siblings.

One day Joseph went to check on his
brothers as they tended their sheep. As his
brothers saw him approaching, they quickly
conspired to kill him. However, rather than be
responsible for his death, they decided to sell
Joseph as a slave to a caravan of merchants
from another country.

Life Reflection

It is hard to imagine that being sold
into slavery could turn out to be a
blessing, as we will discover when we
study Joseph's life further. Remember
the saying, "Hindsight is better than
foresight"? Can you think of a situation that started out as a difficulty but
eventually turned out to be a blessing?

Although it probably wasn't evident to Joseph as he traveled from his homeland to Egypt on a slave caravan, God had not forsaken him. Joseph's trip to Egypt was part of God's divine plan, as was the purchase of Joseph by Potiphar, an officer of Pharaoh and captain of the guard (Genesis 39:1).

In the midst of very trying circumstances, God was with Joseph. "And the LORD was with Joseph, and he was a prosperous man; and he was in the house of his master the Egyptian" (Genesis 39:2). It didn't take long for Potiphar to realize that the favor of God was upon Joseph: "And his master saw that the LORD was with him, and that the LORD made all that he did to prosper in his hand" (Genesis 39:3). "And Joseph was a goodly person, and well favoured" (Genesis 39:6).

Just when things seemed to be improving for Joseph, he was faced with another difficult situation—Potiphar's wife tried to seduce him. But Joseph refused her offer. The favor of God upon his life was more important than a fleeting pleasure. Joseph chose to maintain his integrity before God and did not allow temptation to turn into sin. His response to the temptress was this: "How then can I do this great wickedness, and sin against God?" (Genesis 39:9).

But even though Joseph refused, his difficult situation was not resolved. Potiphar's wife harassed him, entrapped him, and then lied against him to her husband. Potiphar believed her lies and had Joseph thrown in prison.

It seemed things were going from bad to worse for Joseph, but God was still with him. Because of Joseph's right living, he kept the favor of God even in prison: "But the LORD was with Joseph, and showed him mercy, and gave him favour in the sight of the keeper of the prison" (Genesis 39:21).

Life Reflection

Sometimes when we decide to do what is right, it seems things get worse instead of better. Has this ever happened to you? Did you feel discouraged? Sometimes things have to get worse before they get better. And this is where we learn to trust God— that He knows our situation, and that He will work all things together for our good. Read Psalm 37:3-5 and Proverbs 3:5-6.

Joseph was eventually released from prison and promoted to Pharaoh's court because of dreams that he interpreted for the king's baker and butler, and then for Pharaoh himself. "And Pharaoh said unto his servants, Can we find such a one as this is, a man in whom the Spirit of God is? And Pharaoh said unto Joseph, Forasmuch as God hath shewed thee all this, there is none so discreet and wise as thou art: thou shalt be over my house, and according unto thy word shall all my people be ruled: only in the throne will I be greater than thou" (Genesis 41:38-40).

Joseph's interpretation of Pharaoh's dream revealed that there was to be a severe famine in the land, and it described the plan whereby they could store grain to survive. Joseph was selected as the overseer of the project.

The happy ending to the story is that Joseph's entire family was spared from starvation because of the grain stored in Egypt. Joseph forgave his brothers for their misdeeds and was reconciled to them and to his father.

After many years, Joseph understood that the difficulties he had faced were all a part of God's plan (Genesis 45:5-8). Yet through every trial and difficult circumstance, Joseph kept the favor of God upon his life.

The Word in My Life

Joseph was favored by his natural father and by his Heavenly Father, yet his life was filled with many disappointments and difficult situations. However, throughout every situation Joseph maintained his character, his integrity, and his relationship with God. Consequently, in each difficult place he found himself in, Joseph still had the favor of God upon his life. Acts 7:9-10 gives a short synopsis of Joseph's life. Let's read it together:

> "And the patriarchs, moved with envy, sold Joseph into Egypt: but God was with him, and delivered him out of all his afflictions, and gave him favour and wisdom in the sight of Pharaoh king of Egypt; and he made him governor over Egypt and all his house."

Life Reflection

You, like Joseph, may be facing a difficult situation—financial trouble, health problems, marital situations, or emotional distress—but with God's Spirit in your life, you can overcome any difficulty. Read and then try to memorize Philippians 4:13. You can do all things through Christ who gives you strength! Remember that God's favor in your life can turn bitter experiences into beautiful blessings.

The key to God's continual blessing and favor is righteousness, or "right living," through the power of the Holy Spirit. Proverbs 14:9 says, "Fools make a mock at sin: but among the righteous there is favour." We are not righteous in or of ourselves, but through the sacrifice of Jesus Christ at Calvary, who gave His life that we might be able to live life more abundantly. "Who his own self bare our sins in his own body on the tree, that we, being dead to sins, should live unto righteousness" (I Peter 2:24).

When you repent of your sins, are baptized in Jesus' name, and receive the gift of the Holy Ghost, you become a new creature in Christ Jesus. "Therefore if any man be in Christ, he is a new creature: old things are passed away; behold, all things are become new" (II Corinthians 5:17). The "new you" is "after God . . . created in righteousness and true holiness" (Ephesians 4:24).

In order for us to continue to live righteously, we must make right choices. The power of the Holy Spirit within us enables us to discern between right and wrong. The Holy Spirit is given to lead and guide us into all truth (John 16:13). It is important that we daily seek God for direction in everything that we do (Proverbs 3:6). He will give us wisdom to make good decisions and right choices. Ephesians 5:9 says, "For the fruit of the Spirit is in all goodness and righteousness and truth."

Life Reflection

In every difficult situation in his life, Joseph continually made right choices—choices that honored God. And his choices brought God's favor to his life.

As a new creation in Christ, you too must learn to make right choices as the Spirit of God leads you. His Spirit manifests Itself in your conscience, like a gentle nudge, urging you to do the right thing.

"WWJD—What Would Jesus Do?" is a popular slogan of our day. But more than just a slogan, it is a simple way to determine whether you are doing the right thing or not. Just ask yourself, "What would Jesus do?" "Is this a place He would go?" "Is this something I would do if Jesus were here with me?" If you can answer "yes" to each question, you are on the right track. If you happen to make a wrong choice, quickly ask God to forgive you and determine to listen to His voice more carefully the next time. His Word promises that "If we confess our sins, he is faithful and just to forgive us our sins, and to cleanse us from all unrighteousness" (I John 1:9).

(Recommended Reading: *In His Steps* by Charles M. Sheldon. This Christian classic shows how the question, "What would Jesus do?" will cause us to evaluate our actions with a new perspective.)

As you learn to make right choices each and every day of your life, the blessings will come. Some blessings come as a by-product of God's grace in your life and His favor upon you. Other blessings come as a direct result of your faithful obedience to the principles in the Word of God. Proverbs 11:27 says, "He that diligently seeketh good procureth favour." And Proverbs 12:2 says, "A good man obtaineth favour of the LORD."

Life Reflection

Read Psalm 1:1-3.

List the things a man or woman should do to be blessed (verses 1-2).

List the blessings of obedience mentioned in verse 3.

Discuss ways to directly apply this Scripture passage to your life.

Psalm 5:12 says, "For thou, Lord, wilt bless the righteous; with favour wilt thou compass him as with a shield." If you live righteously, God will surround you with His favor as with a shield. His favor will protect you—as a shield—from the difficult situations you face. Psalm 34:19 gives us this promise: "Many are the afflictions of the righteous: but the Lord delivereth him out of them all."

Life is seldom easy, and trouble and hardship happen to us all. But you can rest assured that:

- **The love of your Heavenly Father is constant and unconditional.** "The Lord hath appeared of old unto me, saying, Yea, I have loved thee with an everlasting love: therefore with lovingkindness have I drawn thee" (Jeremiah 31:3).
- **His plan for your life is one filled with hope and purpose.** "For I know the plans I have for you," declares the Lord, "plans to prosper you and not to harm you, plans to give you hope and a future" (Jeremiah 29:11, NIV).
- **His desire is to fill your life with good things.** "But as it is written, Eye hath not seen, nor ear heard, neither have entered into the heart of man, the things which God hath prepared for them that love him" (I Corinthians 2:9).

As God's favor was upon those we have studied—the Israelite people, Esther, Mary, and Joseph—as well as many we did not have time to mention, so is His favor upon you. The angel's message to Mary can be your message today: "thou that art highly favoured, the Lord is with thee: blessed art thou among women" (Luke 1:28).

Life Reflection

This Bible study has led you on a journey to find God's favor:

- ❧ To acknowledge your need of His favor in your life.
- ❧ To learn that you should seek God's favor upon your life through prayer.
- ❧ To know that His favor can be felt through the salvation experience of repentance, water baptism in Jesus' name, and the in-filling of the Holy Ghost.
- ❧ To understand that you can keep God's favor in your life on a daily basis through Spirit-led obedience to His Word.

A Prayer from the Word

Lord, You are my strength and my shield; my heart trusts in You, and I am helped. My heart greatly rejoices and I will praise You with a song. I will praise You: for You have heard me, and have become my salvation.

You are my God, and I will give You thanks; You are my God, and I will exalt You. I will give You thanks, for You are good; Your love endures forever.

You are a refuge for the oppressed, a stronghold in times of trouble. Those who know Your name will trust in You, for You, LORD, have never forsaken those who seek You.

You will direct my steps according to Your Word.

And I am confident that the good work You have begun in me, You will carry on to completion until the day of Christ Jesus.

(Paraphrased from Psalm 28:7; Psalm 118:21, 28-29; Psalm 9:9-10; Psalm 119:133; Philippians 1:6.)

ೞ

More to Life . . . for this week

Memorize this verse: II Corinthians 2:14

Read this passage: II Corinthians 12:7-10

Answer this question: Did Paul, the writer of this passage, suffer hardship and difficulties? Did he allow them to keep him from serving Christ? Paul's areas of weakness were opportunities for God to show Himself strong. Think of a weak area in your life. Can you trust God to show Himself strong on your behalf?

Apply this to your life: If you have not yet experienced the infilling of the Holy Ghost, continue to pray for it. Try to incorporate the "What Would Jesus Do" principle into your life. Keep a journal of the important decisions you make and what effect they have on your life. Do not be discouraged by any circumstance or difficulty that you face as you serve Christ. If you trust Him, He will work everything out for your good.

Have you found God's favor? Reflect on the progress you have made as you have studied each lesson. Think of a woman you know who needs God's favor in her life. Make plans to share this Bible study with her.

Notes

Notes

Notes

Notes

Notes

Women of the Word Commission

Joy Haney

Gwyn Oakes

Mary Loudermilk

Beth Dillon

Gayla Baughman

Julie Long

Renee Flowers

Anne Suarez